Recycled Explosions

Recycled Explosions

Chera Hammons

INK
BRUSH
PRESS

ISBN: 978-0-9909452-4-6
Library of Congress Control Number: 2016936169

Cover Painting: Thomas Moran, "Sunset in Mid Ocean," 1904
Manufactured in the United States

Ink Brush Press
Austin and Dallas

Acknowledgments

I am grateful to the editors of the following publications for publishing some of the poems now in this book.

Amaranthine Hour, Jacar Press
2 River View
Blow
The Cherry Blossom Review
Concho River Review
Connotation Press
Hospital Drive
Improbable Worlds (Mutabilis Press)
The Pitkin Review
Red River Review
subTerrain
whimperbang

Poetry Collections from Ink Brush Press

For information on these and other Ink Brush Press books go to
www.inkbrushpress.com

For
D and all that we will do next

CONTENTS

III. Light and Heat

IV. The Way It Radiates

I. Accelerant

America

We told ourselves it was the most beautiful
horizon we'd ever seen, and to keep
our mouths closed. We told the others nothing but how

sometimes we couldn't help it, were not to blame,
with a mother raised by Religion and
gender and toothpaste, and a father who
tried to keep us out of the living room, hulking, humming

like the old icebox shut green and filthy
before our kitchen became a dishwasher
garbage disposal and other conveniences.

Safe in the lead paint and bed the electric
stove was our home, watching while
we slept in fields of foxes like wildlife,

harvesting trees that crackled and danced.
Our inheritance was not entailed:
free rusty sinew, but mostly

comfort, for us—that our Lean Cuisine
heats in minutes, that nothing

is on television and the Salisbury steak is
a little frozen in the middle,
but the edges are done.

Playing outside, their noises in the sandbox muffled,
tainted with acquired soil,
we constructed landscapes with sticky hands, all shapes,

the alien mud here in grains in the wash,
and leaving Micro Machines and G.I. Joes
decaying into homes for beetles.

Even those ghosts don't judge us,
voices only sand or water

where the ocean smoothed them over like
ice crystals blooming over old chicken
in the refrigerator,

the Pledge pine smell and grocery store
flowers and what has been left out of children.

This city, undisplaced by secrets,
the grab-something-for-lunch and morning traffic,
forgets when the bombs went off.

It was a clear day with nothing unremarkable.
Our burden becomes that of no history, of possessing nothing old.

Prelapse

We do not know that we are naked. The
pale rose with its burnished tips is
sheathed in color, bare like us, able to
bleed with sometimes afterthought. It is a
sun disciple, pulls heat in, reflects in
itself a demi-god.

It is not the cutting of stems; it is
not the lifting of the sole or roll of the
heel; it is not the cry from the air that takes
flight from the sparrow into the hawk. Snow
fading into snow greyly, pricks of sky between
eyelashes, the green sleep of trees with
the wind around them: nothing knows like the
crystalline shape still holding water in curves,
the smear of leaves on its side from old charges.

Fingers mute the impressions on coins. Hands
used to work wrestle emptiness weighed
by a desert, gripped in Godhead and stairs
climbed in dreams. With ear to the ground

Israel lies, listening for footsteps or the
noise of eroding rock, the hold of roots
in the sand, anything that hits where he
hits and stays. He waits
for the awakening of water, the run of
rain silent until it finds surfaces.
The falling itself is soundless.

Local News

As our bare feet slapped the sidewalk
we sugared the ants with ice cream
from the peddler who knew our names.
The trebles of his square truck and the cicadas
taught us the way to recognize July.

I notice the seasons, even now—
streets shimmering, the smell of water in the sun,
grass clippings drifting down the curb.

I remember the girl who lived one house down,
her bicycle and inscrutable older brother.

We were all the same kind of people.
I knew what was mine then too,
all the law and kingdom of a dead end street.

Now we bump into each other during the holidays,
narrowing from the runways tired of delays
and navigating interstates we have traveled so often
we know all the cleanest stations.

Our parents live in the same houses,
behind those split cottonwoods streaked with sap
that congeals to amber pearls in the snow.

The few trees shake from lumbering through their own weight,
treacherous and sacred as our bewildered bodies,
which are this age for the first time.

We say it's good to see you, would love to catch up
but we don't plan to be in town for long.

Those who read weather will tell you
to leave early, if you do not want to stay.

This year there will be another hard winter,
and there are other beds that won't wait for us.

Visiting Aunt Lori in East Texas

The last time I saw her, she hadn't learned
how to forget her baldness;
like a new sort of brother in an old faith,
she still weighed her order
to the way of the world outside.

Wrapped in a threadbare robe
she padded to the mirror
as we lay in spare beds,
 and she creaked over the boards of
warped wood, knots toothy
with mold, under a roof
swayed with the humidity.
Her fingers explored her scalp
the way we rubbed our faces when
the spores and pollen in the rooms
powdered our sweated skin.

She was too thin.
We had breakfast together
without speaking of the paradigm
of the nightly light on the hallway floor,
sat chewing as the persistent forest sent roots
to push the pier-and-beam foundation apart
under the sunny green kitchen
and the rally of the tea kettle.

Aunt Lori wanted to love
a man just one more time.
She thought she had enough
of her reflection left to do it.
My mother didn't want me to listen
to the unwholesome talk of the sickness
and sent me past the screen door,
its eyelet swinging
and the paint chipping behind.

I could still hear the house
from the wild blackberry thicket
and the grey-slumped barn,
slick with lichen's primordial thumbs
clinging greedy to the rotted planks.
From the rusty swing I heard
my mother's voice and hers fluttering,
two moths beating their dust
against that blank window on the yard,
trying to find a way back to what they knew.
It was unlike the other summers, when
golden and warm, flower-smell from the shower
before she went out for the night,
 Aunt Lori pushed me in the comfortable
creaking chains in which I rocked.

She laughed then haloed with sun and tanned.
With each arc over the pine needles
an echo called like hidden crickets,
small rub of bravery to tell across walls
the temperature of the unfamiliar rooms
where we would begin to try to sleep.

1990

Rustling through the cattails by the road
hard-dusted with sun and shining
around the horse's fetlocks,
I passed under the laughing tree's
clacking limbs

and bowed into the field that wasn't mine
but wasn't fenced, stepping over the
curled wire that had fallen low,
and it waved me in.
I was lilting among golden maize

as tall as my ears. It parted with hidden lions
that moved the stalks as they padded.
The spooked horse, whose instinct was my own,
could hear them growl too.
But I was safe there. It was what I knew
in the days before I had any knitting bones:
I could sit any pony, I was sure of it,

but especially that one, lovely,
sunny and lithe, smoky-skinned.

At night I lived in the morning's sound
as I sat at the smudged glass and wicker table
with the family that still had dinner together.

There was war in the desert.
In the dark den that waited for us,
the television shelled crack-crack-crack.
We listened for the news to change to weather
as the tired chairback crackled, worn,
under my younger brother's leaning,
and my parents told us, their daily ritual:
eat everything on your plates.

The Pictures Are On A Tilt

The pictures are on a tilt, shaken by wind, a hand that came in
under the door, teased the fire, and scattered papers. Van Gogh lost
his mother, his ear, and finally his balance on my wall.

Drops of stars gather in the corner of the frame,
catch on the cathedral, slide off mountains and the
tops of houses, leave ripples around their empty spaces.
Midnight pushes forward, black. The villagers do not
feel the valley spinning, do not see it, but hear it creak.
The ground falls up, the buildings tremble, lights jump
to life in the sanctuary; stained glass blocks the cracking
roads, turns the world outside into Virgin Mary blue.

The left side needs only a lift, the right perhaps a lowering,
and all of it an extra nail to keep it from rocking again. Just that.
It is not unwhole. But it lacks realization; it is a house forgetting
the holes in the old plaster, the water-stain on the ceiling;
pale shed skin of a snake left on green lawn.
And then, too, windows are not doors.

Stars slide down the bell-tower, drip from trees, surrender for nothing.
They leave no face, not a footprint or shadow.
They are not recognition, reflection, or alarm,
the small half-frightened voices of a village routine.

When all has melted, no gaps appear. The picture is not unwhole.
Only, sinking, stars watch traces of themselves disappear behind them,
a sort of comet: faces of an imaginary congregation in an oil church
lit by moon; a painting, in a narrow frame, sliding out.

Let Me Give You a Light

The woman relaxes, settles back with
ash at the end of her tongue, a fire

that sits gently at her lips—she
rolls it in her fingers and sighs,

watching the grey afterthoughts of flame in the air.
The light at the tip of her nose is a firefly

bit of pale, life among its kin in the dark bar.
Smoke hangs in the room

like the clink of pitchers and voices.
9 to 5 and other wages have molded

the leather-imitation stools to fit every shape.
The spark in the dark speaks a self-inhaling smolder

like the laughter of tired friends at an old joke—
shining, aging, dying at the dim and crowded counter.

Wolf-Tongue

You dream of a shining being making bright things,
and that is when the moon falls.

Fear is featureless, in the shape of a man. The light falls.
You open your throat to catch it;
the darkness whispers *Prophesy, but do not
Love*. The dark god of dark creatures spreads your
teeth, saying, *Sing*, saying, *Do this wordlessly*.

The night has scoured you to sinew
with its waiting. *Say that you are waiting*,
disembodied lung, hidden speech, black
Instrument—come in through the cracks where
the house has settled. Come out from the
low places into the airtight room.

Dogs listen to the ground open. They
worry the sleeping chambers where their masters
rest. They can smell the last breath
leaving, pulling the warmth under skin out through every wall.

You feel the wilderness of your descent and
Stand. When this simplicity of speech falters, you hear
the shadows move; the hollows of the fields
lie bare and drying in the sun.

There is a pause when he sees what he has
Illuminated. The earth sparkles as it moves.
Its surface shines with clouds.

The voice says *Sing, and hold it there*.

After the Famous Poet's Reading at the University

The bells in the towers around the parking lot clanged and shivered,
 though it was 8:40 at night, and they had no reason for it.
It was warmer outside than it had been in the theater.
A girl danced in front of the headlights of a car,

but stopped, embarrassed, when she saw people walking out.
The air was fresher outside, too, the trees newly leafed and resting,
and something about the stillness of the air around the green life
        shimmered,
though it was the poem with the red backpack that struck me most:

how he described the dark splotches on it from the rain in California.
While I had listened to it, the sun was setting,
and the grackles that had been umbrellaed and parading in the grass
already folding somewhere to sleep.

I thought about how, because poets never come here, no one had known
when to applaud, and everyone had waited for someone else to start,
the way I would sit waiting for the cars to leave the parking lot.
Inside I had sat in front of a man who smelled like garlic and beer

and laughed in all the wrong places while he and an engineer joked
about how students with low GPAs dream of going to med school.
Overall, I felt I had been sitting down too long,
and around the bewilderment of the bells

and the girl shimmying in and out of lightbeams,
felt glad to be outside again, and glad the poet himself seemed kind,
when I met him, though he had spelled my name with an *S*.

On Monet's *Deux Vases de Chrysanthèmes*

Not Yet, he says with red shades
      (I will not say a little at a time)

He tells you Now, and you ripen
With strokes of eglantine fervor.

Nothing drops but an orange shadow
on the table and light stretching
as he looks and moves.

He says Speak in this language, with this tongue
arched, uncrowned, almost a prince.

You are a ghost, a ghost—the
Mouth meant Spirit, which was
the crackling in the branches—

Hands that would tear the stems
undo and remake themselves. The
eyes have no scales left, but

there is paint: *Argenteuil, la berge
En fleurs*, becoming *Bleed like this
and have no history.*

Gold dances in the lifeless flanks, the creature
mutely sets its ears (we will go down to see)
—Light the lamps, cover the garden with leaves.

There is time, and I cut purple faces from the
green out of this soil; from a handful of dust
alongside translucency, vein-watering, and rain.

      We could throw paper flowers into the snow
and watch the petals wet. We could be
awake through midnight making them.

Another amaranthine hour, feet grey and
the door opens on the floor
with a trapezoid of light; I am sleeping I am sleeping
"Goodnight," he says.

The cold parts of the feet linger (goodbye to those who
built and lay in the shadow *Meules, fin de l'été,
effet du matin*).

The impression fills overnight
Softly. You are made in that red mixture.

Your corners are red.
Some would take off their shoes
    for such holiness.

Train Graffiti

An unmarked train has never rested.
Too many people aching for something to claim leave
their names on the empty coal hoppers and steel boxes
in the slanted shadows of still cranes and blackened chimneys
while fires burn and streets sleep.

Flashing by fields after a furlough, rolling initials
flick across the bottoms of the cars,
an impression of sunglowed blossoms
to jackrabbits shaded in mesquite.
The train rides around its cargo swaying,
heavy like some ocean's freighter.
The iron and wood of the rails hear stories
of the heat, its weight,
while its machinery swells with dappled grace.
The rails thunder with the friction of its rush,
and the colors above the wheels toss and shimmer
as the train flashes past the blinking lights

of crossings, slowing through the towns.
        When it stops, it is vandalism.

Old Laguna

I have never turned deliberately
toward the ruins of the pueblo that rises
like a ridged yellow thumbnail
past the interstate mesas,
chipping moon,

but I notice it from far off
with a devoted
aversion.

Unkempt it grinds the sand
to the cirrus,
and once scattered
its people,
who dropped their
bread and water
as it fell and left them
to sell pinion nuts
from red and gray primer-coated
Chevy trucks by the closed bridge.

It seems a place best avoided,
an iniquitous tattoo
on the flank of the Sangre de Cristos.
The cracked sandstone crawls like cuticles
to the empty windows;
the heat presses wrinkled reptiles
to the walls.

Maybe we end this way too—
dry and unexfoliated,
not open to visitors,
crumbling without even any sort
of war-glory, or any clean
white tip,

a silence starry travelers pass
on their way to other places.

Singlefooting
to J.V.

In my hands there is memory,
binds of bones and blood.
The heat rising from the caliche smokes
and swirls from blue feet,
a cadence and thrust on the still street,
making pebbles scatter, creaks
with our footfalls. This is something
I have only claimed
to make the road better for a while.
We pass trees that lyricize the wind,
with borrowed birds in them lilting,
the leaves whispering, trees talking in tree
language. My will is in the teeth, the guide
in a land shining with newness. The cheekpieces
clink as tangles split over the brow.

Don't start at rabbits—we are greater than they;
ours is the balance of opposite instinct that
exists between fingers, knees, and
unscientific explanations.
I have your grace. I run as fast as you.
From far off, the low sweet lyric of a train,
unseen machine that makes us dance with agitation.
We jump at the quail that appear from our feet
because we are fine-spirited.

Let us not create anything remarkable, too much missed.
From these veins, blue memories swell into the
salt-sweet smell of sweat, a crested neck lathered,
white foam, like late autumn, a transitory enchantment.
Here, more than what is usual, the wind fills my throat,
the fields are clean, the hot road is swept
of dust by unrestraining gale.
For an hour I am a nomad.

Why do people sing? – Why do whales?
I push the horse into the wall of my
hands. I gather him in my arms like a tiger.

Checking the Cattle at Indian Hill

When I pull up to the gate, I see that the antelope have arrived
to graze within the herd, though the cows keep their wet noses buried
in the wheat, unconcerned by those jubilant golden heads
crowned with their forked mahogany.
Grass-hardened and wire-scarred, the wild creatures have spread
through the lowing blanket of the cows, and seem comfortable
in the gentle shelter of thick brown bodies,
the rhythmic clips of stems.

I roll down the window to see without its tint
the way they leave, breathless and startling
in blinding flashes of white you can see from miles away.
Rushing with the same kind of path
the wind makes moving over the Llano Estacado,
they dive under the bottom strand of barbed wire.
A new calf watches around the flank of its peaceful mother,
but doesn't find in their flight the right way to fear,
 or see what makes the antelope run, or why.

Nesting Boxes

A snake has been
after the eggs again,
stealing them from our Rhode Island Reds
as they chase cabbage butterflies in the yard,
empty-headed.

Unhurried, slurred, soft-spoken, it must wait
in the shade at the edge
of the chicken wire,
coiled by the sparkling
lattice, split tongue slicking the air,
watching the hens parade
into the dusty morning.
It must slide sideways quick
into their warm boxes,
unhinging its jaw to fit around
that hot brown burden.

It is, for a while, content
with an oval throat, the sliding
soft down its belly.
We do not know how close our day goes to it.
The chickens scratch unwary of concern,
used to their vanishing labors.

In the morning we might find
shed skin spread pale, slit
down the middle as if the eggs
have hatched from its paper stomach,

the wage that its appetite has paid.
It is easy enough to go near then,
emptied and drying, released from its sins.

Anvil Clouds

Someone left the horse out again.
The light in the barn is an empty
bulb swinging on its cord
in the driving wind
where he should stand sleeping
through the drift and hush of owls.
It is easy for summer dusk to
forget horses, when
they are lazy in the grass
and in no hurry to shuffle in
from their lukewarm golden sea.

We should have seen it coming;
clouds boiled over all day. There
were warnings. But it broke
and now the horse
is lost in a thunderhead's mouth
in a field that opens its fevered throat
to catch the pelting rain.
The air sizzles on the hot iron
of the sky.

The horse must be standing
in those acres somewhere,
beaten with many tiny heels,
unable to escape.
His back is not used
to the weight of this force and he will shy
and slip through the first storm of the season

surprised though one way or another every day
teaches him something else to expect.
In my slicker I feel sheathed
in sound, and follow the posts to
hooves whose eyes are rims of moon,
plunging at the edge of the fence
through gap-toothed lightning
and slowly hand out I step, soft.

There is the sucking cold mud.
As we face each other we shiver
with something
that isn't the temperature
though we are both bedraggled wet.
I know if I slip he will spook
and we will lose ourselves again in storm.
If there is no bringing him in
we will be finished, the night too much
for me to stay out in.
The hail bullies us to lower our heads
but in the reaching mud
the horse's breathing arrives to pimple my skin.
The pelting on the tin of the shed swallows the water
with the brown pasture dust
as it falls through the rusted punctures of screws
when I lead him back.

It's not the first time someone has caught
a horse in a storm.
They are so often drawn to the fences,
guided mostly in flashes
and you get to know all the tricks to catch one,
how in darkness when the earth shakes
they want move a little closer until a hand is on a halter
and they remember there is shelter.
That if they can make themselves be still enough,
someone will arrive who wants
to take another one in.

Fledglings

Some say it's a myth, that the parents
won't care for their young
once they sense humanity on them,
that they will stop feeding them
and watch them shrink to bones
while they stuff the others,
the untouched ones, with worm-meal.

In the spring winds, when a few get shaken out
and left to bloat untended,
or to be taken away by foxes,
or carried piece-by-piece to fill red ant dens,
I pretend not to see them in the grass
helpless, unable to hold up their naked heads,
but still living, wild wills full of hope
because dying is not the same as dead.

Once they're on the ground, it's too late.
Don't touch them, I tell myself.
Don't reach up and replace them,
don't get close enough to see that they breathe
or think about the ease
of putting something so small back in its place.

What is wild is wild.
I have read over and over
that my help may just as well harm,
and the many other reasons I shouldn't interfere
in the spheres of untamed creatures.

They have their ways.
I have heard it so often, it must be true.

And we have ours.

Praise

Between the planting and the harvest,
the bread that feeds your children

begins to be more than just a swishing
against the ankles of the shortcut takers

and the neighbor's flea-bit dog.
It becomes more itself the taller and drier

and yellower it grows.
It whispers, begins to watch for you,

to know your routines in its rhythms,
to welcome the walkers of the rows

and plowers of the fallow,
the irrigators, engine-runners,

the frighteners of cottontails.
You live together in the furrows.

Somewhere before the harvester comes,
when your hopes and those

of the spring wheat are the same,
you call to each other with one language.

Then like a jealous mother
you overspeak the field.

When the light dies out the field without the light
is still warm and tough,

richer than it was, as the dirt cloys like promises
under the heels of your home-coming.

The ponies are shifting their weight in the dark,
the crickets Marco-Poloing between the stalks,

and the ground-birds rustling to a roost tame as hens.
The knowledge of farming is yours

as much as your stories, is in your names.
You are born into it this way,

and then you have to stay.
You have to be a thresher, a journaler of bad years,

a destroyer of the voices you have loved.

You have to write the sounds in another order
and make them into songs.

II. How It Starts to Ignite

Prometheus

Bound to the mountaintop he watches fires hatch beneath him,
appearing like timid stars, more showing the deeper the dark.
Soon the night will be alive with tiny sparks. The forest will
flicker. Men will warm their hands.

They called her Pandora. Her veil hid her beauty:

All greatness is made of fire: its heat, its cat's-eye brightness,
its blue intensity, its search for dry fuel.
Fire is men living, alive and tight inside themselves,
their lungs filled with air, their hearts against their skin,
rough-knuckled, with their wives warm beside them.
He feels his prison and watches the ground ignite.

Wait, they told her, but she moved her wrist,
and we saw something like bats:

Their flame his flame, their smoke his too,
from his perch on the cliff the light
shines like candles seen across a room,
fading out in the soft gray, orange circles and blue centers.
His breath is the breath that coaxed their life, his hand the one that
spread the sun from wick to wick.

Pandora, Pandora, what have you done? The human race
will always regret you:

The wise, the foresightful, the shameless and artful,
held resigned by irons against granite, against time, against pain,
holds his eye to the ground below him. There stands Pandora,
who has let the night and its black out with a rush.
He loves her for it. The fires look like stars.
It was right in my hands, she said. How couldn't I?

His face wavers with light. Like fireflies in summer, he thinks.
A million new fireflies in as many Junes.

A hundred thousand streetlights. Bread rising in the ovens.
A thousand yellow living room windows. Garden lanterns.
Fire, he laughs. I gave them fire!

Oh what will become of us! she cried

Holy Days

I, too, have spoken of the endlessness I may walk into

and of knowing that "I am afraid that I will lose faith,"
I say, as if I think that it is all up to me.

If I do not take the body, it is only that
others too are in my stomach like dandelions
because spring is what I meant and what I thought was growing,

...but there are no transitions here, nothing without yellow petals
breaking its demeanor.

They have run away with me, and I remember reading

that the holy man's hair did not turn white, but his face
was radiant, they said,
and so he wore a veil to cover it.

The shadow slants at my feet a sightless reflection,
and I wet my toes in black portraits.

If I do not fit, then I will dig deeper in.
The sun finds itself in the shining eyes

(everything turning its face toward something brighter)

until the blossoming is lured after it to the dark ocean.
It will be tangled singing in the connections,
dragging its gold behind it, and dropping feathers.

Religion is forgotten the same as history—
the way rain slips down the stems of grass
where I might have walked barefoot, and the oak tree
inside the acorn knows that

uncurling leaves or the weight of earth splits the shell,
but it does not know which it will break into:
the sunlight or the teeth.

Atmosphere

Whether swimming in water or air,
some atmosphere will get you.
Lanky quick like ostriches
the infamous grackles chase low-
drifting moths
soft like discarded down.

For the sunflowers, it's open,
invisible but not hello—
the bees, come rest your feet in me,
dandelion, sweeter we are to the sky.

You know, too, that breath, the antediluvian sea
and evaporated bodies, and what's richer after a rain
from what appeared to lose its way
5 or 10 inches from its tunneled grass.
The earthworms twist on the sidewalk as
their speech dries end-to-end,
plea Mercy of us, the cousins of birds,
who step over the places they lie.

Parable

The merchant's camel
was far too large
to sew with, so
he melted his daughter's
jewelry into a needle
and drove its newly fashioned
point into the dunes.
It arched over the road
a silver eye and
people brought their caravans
from the desert to ride
through it.
The children
liked to watch the glint of
the sun in the
parabola
as they passed under—
they saw themselves
strange-shaped
moving with a specter of light
down the curves
at a pace smoother than
their mounts were plodding,
colored bundles
safe-rolled tight
and shining.
Some of the men squatted
so that only sky was in the oval,
recognizing its greatest aspect,
but most went through
so they could tell the wives
who bartered in the market
of seeing their kind of miracle.

Why Poetry

Because a good poem, like the Sphinx
(licking its complacent lips,
purring riddles), can
nonchalantly
kill a man with one flick of its great paw—
Or, it may sit over him and stare, swishing its tail,
smiling in a way so human, it's terrifying,
letting him see every line of the terrible golden expression
before the monster devours him—
Unless it makes a king of him instead

Jacob Wrestles

The way he tells the story,
it was not that he awakened—
the night is often interrupted by
wailing babies, dogs bickering,
the water sound of wind
whirling across the shining grit—
but how it happened, in his solitary camp,
to hands rough like his own, which catch on
rough-spun cloth and wool,
and a body straight splintered like his,
polished and sand-taut as a bone
that could spool around itself the sleep
into which he had been woven.

That night he had slept too far from me.
As he stepped from his robes he was alone
with another nomad and the desert
that must at last have been mysterious.
Fright did not change what the sand
hid from him—he has strangled
lionesses as brute as zebras.
It was not his weakness echoing
from the rocks—he is hardest-knotted
of the entire tree of his people.
Maybe he really didn't know why he so felt
his own pulse in his throat.

The way he tells it, he struggled with
what could have been his own reflection
until the sun wavered over the huddled dunes,
and there were the sounds of river birds
and the far-away camp of family stirring
on the other bank, where he saw me,
straining to understand what was happening.
Then their tired feet slipped, sand burned sandal-less heels,
and panting they released each other.

Our fathers taught us one kind of obedience,
but who hasn't wondered if there are others?
He claims that those whom God cannot overwhelm limp.

I still don't know what other spirit he embraced.
When I ask him at night he will not speak
the name of that stranger any longer,
saying that to name it would be apostasy.

Vintages

I am more native than anyone,
even members of the earlier tribes
who knew ahead the same visions
of the lumbering earth rising from the sea,

who heard first the way
the land split apart, brimming
with rivers, to become a wilderness.

This country is my father, twisted
and woody, clinging to fences
and trying to climb frail and veined
in the beginning, ascending:

hiding nothing vital from me.
Flowers bloomed and introverted green,
stretching from the shadows of Ararat.
My family remembers, too,

how we thumped against the musky sides
of camels that crossed the wastelands
and in the holds of ships that cradled us
in creaking oak, much as I am now.

Always the soil was where we
became again ourselves,
stretched as deep as we were wide,
slowly tilling the feral rocky fields.

Shaped by drought and Paradise
our skins ripen firm to pale and royal.
Plucked we are carried in basins,
for the first time finding our own voices,

soon after pressed again together.
We wait in barrels in stone caves
while midwives turn us in our wombs
and remind us of breath and of the split.

The earlier harvests know a little less than me,
the later will know something more.

There were others we have heard of
who have accomplished amazing feats.
A generation is said to have sprung where there
was only water; it had no stem.

These are the few questions
we think to ask, and how
we filter away the time before we are released
once again to the bright air. We worry,
as brothers soon to be divided,

we will find we have become too new
for the old skin that some will try to pour us into.

Paseo Del Volcan

An ancient shift in
the outer crust
has caused three volcanoes
to stop Albuquerque
from traveling west.
Natives call them the Sisters
as if those brooding landscapes
knitting trees together with
wrinkled roots
and brewing sulphur
to warm veined hands
are people they went to school
with or elderly neighbors.
Clicking pine needles
in an unbothered homeland
they seem content to shelter
gossiping coyotes.
Hikers lean over the hidden
hearts of molten rock
to discuss the day's weather.
The Sisters have gentle uttered
no cross word to any living animal
for as long as anyone can remember.
Their rest makes mountains of old maids
who hold in grumbling death and all its new land
enough to appease polite company.

How We Look to Mars

When she sees herself
reflected in Earth's seas, the
beauty makes her blush.

Belongings

When we first found I was executor I inventoried
the hand-painted collectible figurines
and old school papers
and wondered whether to donate, discard, or box them.
There was china chipped but still good,
a Rosie the Riveter jewelry box,
and a Cherokee great grandmother, gazing benignly
through a penchant for baking and divine intuition.

Some items would make good gifts
(to be forwarded, a book only partly read—
a desire for creation—assortment of photographs—
the willingness to buy postage).

The unwanted remains sat untidily out
for passers-by to index:
fat knees, used cancerous tendencies,
emotion leaking through the cardboard
in the neglected yard, guilt you have to
sit on to keep closed.

When I knew they were mine for good
I put them in the attic. The sun faded them,
strange fingerprints, like voices in the roof.

We planned and still to sort them
when the room is full.
I am the same as my mother, with a different vocabulary.

Subdivision

My neighbor walks across her yard in a red skirt
and my dogs bark.

Maybe they are not used to seeing her.
She lives in a big house that oozes money, and it is usually quiet.

She bought it with a settlement and never leaves it.
All she does is pull weeds from between her roses.

I go to work when it is dark and come home when it is dark.
The dogs must see her more than I do, but still they bark.

Maybe they are just not used to seeing her in red.
I have only ever seen her in black sweatpants
and a white sweatshirt. Only on weekends.

Once I saw her in black sweatpants
throwing a bin full of trash over my fence.

I took pictures of her doing it. She waved at me
like there was nothing unusual going on.

To her, I guess there wasn't.

She has a dog, too. When I go outside,
it runs into my yard and growls at my ankles.

She yells *Lady, Lady* but always gives up and ignores what it does
because it ignores her.

When I look into Lady's scrunched up face
I have to choke the urge to chase her back to her yard.

Then I wonder how dogs define who is trespassing.
Do they think what they see is what they should defend?

Lady chases joggers, too.
My dogs watch from behind the fence
and bark at her as she nips at heels.

Maybe they would do that themselves, if I let them run loose.
I don't think they would.
Still, every time the neighbor walks across her yard
in a red skirt, my dogs bark.

You'd think that they'd be used to her by now.

Inverse Sonnet to the Black Dun

Run because you were born knowing how, to
unfold ground as soon as a tired mother
rolled back the sacred dark with her teeth. In
one shudder began a bright story, of

sun and the first shadow cast from weak knees.
Hold it still. I didn't know you, never
sold, yet. With each step becoming effect
spun from a silk thread that shook when you walked,

gait was something you just picked up. Windy
trees and stones that chipped your feet had the same
speech as you then. Your mouth had not yet known

the weight of a bit. That you would be furrowed like the ground.
How we start out not knowing what will be missed,
that each day of survival takes more from us.

Cold Front at Buffalo Lake

The fish were first to go. From one day the algae shallows they were
    used to
bottom-water reversed—too many cloud-covered afternoons, or
    chemicals.
Their gills opened uselessly, mouths gaped red as molten glass. Their
    silver scales
mirrored each other asphyxiating. A crushing buoyancy turned them
    into surface.
The water, without its air and under-shimmering, showed safety to
    hapless mosquitoes.

It is this coolness that draws me here. A desire to document this
    upheaval in the still
shadows, the quiet trees that watched and began growth with their roots
in shells. The lake has dried now to make room for them. Without the
fish it was unreasonable to go on.

At the gate I see no one else has come here. The empty threat of rain,
gray in a land of stillness—this is no place for picnickers or watchers of
    birds. As if everything at the
boundary decided nothing exists today. The trees conspire to drop
    nothing into the grass.
All of them old men waiting out the apocalypse that surely is occurring
    past the highway.
They muffle the outside noises into their branches.

The Hasselblad sticks—can such grayness have enough measure to
reproduce? To say I stole something that was mine in the beginning!
Cottonwoods angled like my sinews. Their disregard for storm
warnings. Their love of the whiting fog. Their voices lost in echoes.

We sometimes beg for lack of color. The fawns that move from in front
of our feet soundlessly. Ageless eyes that touch us with moth-wings.
Outside are prodigies, arrows, watches with tiny strained springs
dictating sunlight (which unbounded makes us immortal):

I wanted life to have edges. Not glass to cut—but it isn't. Here the Peregrines scream to melting sky, melting leaves, shining ponds that vanish after sunrise. They cry how much time have you lost. Waiting down there. Catching the shafts of feathers.

Something needs to fight and tear down. I stayed awake to kill the white dog that stopped his invading. After that I refused making pictures. Like standing, the trees echo where I have been. Stretched thinner as they travel. Like a flashlight into stars.

Like the fish we are here for a day of nothing. The emptiness of love in rotting headstones, the forgotten relatives; the world of moss and rain and rocks. It's a surviving place. From the white shells the only sign of the decayed water, the

green-skinned carp, ghosts in the grass that warn deer of another new winter.

South Rim

It is not where to go as a tourist
out of season. *Winter is a consideration:*
the brochure itself says it, lying
thumbed in the passenger seat.

Be prepared to drive until dusk.
I stand quiet in a coat
that snowmelt has darkened into slate
near the exhale and click of cooling engines.
The fog finds visitors
curling and blowing against the cold.
I can see their breath just enough to find boundaries.
A group of gray pillars
bends under umbrellas, in hoods,
huddled strangers. Maybe they also have read of
warm burros that amble
down the frost-dusted red trails,
the spread skirts of sleeping cliffs
and streams pumping between them
too far away to hear from the rim. I never
expected snow in Flagstaff.

Bring your own water.
The cries of a blackbird sink slow as boulders.
Stay between the edges of the path.
Even the children are silent,
as if they're suspicious of their own noise,
that if they spoke their words would go
trickling off the rocks
past the ages of the earth
and never rescued.

There is a lone rail through the white air
to warn tourists back,
and the gray form of a juniper clawing its way
up the rock closest to where I wait,
that twisted shape the limit of my sight.

Return in better weather.
This view can go on for hours—
the brochure would say to come back, if it knew.

The Sound of Traffic

The summer we watched her die,
we stayed in my aunt's white-sided house
right off the highway.

Inside and out, all we could hear were cars
rushing past to get to places, sirens, impatient horns,
sounds that slid under all of our conversations,
something we couldn't speak loud enough to cover.

They were something we learned to live around.
We didn't talk much at dinner,
didn't sleep well,
turned the TV all the way up in the afternoons.

I could see my aunt even when I didn't want to.
Her room at the end of the hallway
had a French door of clear panels in rows that showed
her shrinking among the sheets.

The door opened with a crystal knob almost too small for your hands.
They don't make them like this anymore,
my mother said as if sharing a secret, fingering it
as its facets glinted and threw light
about the room like a world of diamonds.

I could tell she wanted one like it.
I wanted one, too,
could think of it on my own door, beautiful and cool,
how something like that would change
the way people come into a place.

Later, I tried to find them for my own house,
understood how expensive they are,
and when I held one in my hand
remembered how when we left there, we left everything immaculate.

How the tire swing pendulumed gently in the wind
as the wild blackberries unreached us.

How the place looked abandoned
once we knew we wouldn't return to it.

How we had gone back toward where we had come from:
the unwooded fields six hours north,
the quiet brick house on the cul-de-sac,
the good school district,

the friends who expected us to come back the same
as we had left, a little older, maybe,
a little more concerned, for a while, with living,
but still pretending there could be a way to speak
over all that rushes on.

West Nile

How they ran toward the house. By the end,
anything, even retreat, to beat that high hum,

to get past the familiar sting
in unreachable places,

pinch in the forgotten hollow of soft skin
where fluids of the earlier bird or horse

would lodge above their muscles
while their blood slipped out of them

like black oil from a shale bed.
But the blood quickened as they went,

drew nearer the surface, sweetened sweat
and sharpened that offering.

And when they stopped to wipe their foreheads
they saw they had carried a few with them

all along, began to hit their own bodies in spasms,
and the blood they spilled was their own.

Some mosquitoes disattached sated and opaque,
leaving, not looking back, though taking the children off

drop by drop. And though the full ones had gone,
more arrived to join the tingle of the phantoms.

Slapping their arms and talking, they entered.
Where the mosquitoes had been, little mounds of red

still lifting imperfected their escape,
though they had passed through a doorway to a house

and nothing had followed them inside.

Visiting the Beaches at Normandy

I see them springing from the waves
that break like snow before the plow.
I see them rushing from the foaming sea,
skinny thoroughbreds from the gate.
A strange blindness fills the damp as they charge;
they grope for something to hold in the dark
the way a scared boy reaches for his teddy bear.
How can they be soldiers when they are barely men?
They have fathers, girlfriends, small jobs, goldfish.
Some are just out of college, some just in.
They are greatness not yet out of its tight bud.
They are awkwardness, newness, frightened vivacity,
a flock of gangling, passionate, just-hatched geese—

But their collective, memorialized soul,
the Statue of Youth set at the entrance,
looks like a winged-foot Mercury in bronze,
a regal messenger captured just before it flies.
And the plain white crosses, some with Jewish stars,
are clean and strong, a memorial to innocence,
but the quiet tourists only bow their heads
under the weight of the death of it.

I wonder if field larks quieted their songs in the trees.
I wonder if the air tasted of salt.

Between graves, tour guides whisper the technicalities—
who did this, here, and that, over there, and why;
but there are no technicalities here,
nothing solid or logical—nothing.
I see the waves break. The ghosts leap
from where the future is resting to find it asleep.

The Purple Triangles

Have you heard any news
          from outside?
We are too far gone
   to turn into them
so they don't even try to make us
anymore, those sharp wolves
  whose teeth roll
their cigarettes, who flick
the soggy butts
     into where we wait
bunched   and fading.
          We think of all the other shapes
our shapes could make,
and how god's name came
          to miss its vowels.
          We are lined up,
we are folded into origami geometries
 then crushed in handfuls,
   thrown atop one another, quiet as mutes.
          I think of how we will all
crawl out of it into the sunlight,
          one day,
          how they will finally know
that we were   alive the whole time
inside our gray clothes, grey hair,
and the prayers we sent up with the smoke.
   We had homes. What has changed there?
          It is against my religion
to have a tattoo, but I do.

A Letter from the Manufacturers of Umbrellas to Protesters in the Hong Kong Umbrella Revolution

In response to your claim,
we feel we should warn you:
there are functions an umbrella
was not meant to perform.

Each one, carefully designed by a team of engineers
and lovingly tested in harsh conditions
using time-proven methods,
will faithfully shed anything the heavens throw at it
(within reason).

Clusters of hydrogen and oxygen
atoms, electron arms wrapped around each other
as they plummet from where they were lighter
versions of themselves, won't touch you.

The sun's ultraviolet tides, washing the earth
with its flotsam of radiation, will lap and foam
at the edge of your island of shadow
while you stand in the middle, unscathed.

That being said, there are uses that won't be tolerated.
Take, for example, the blustering wind.
These soft bones weren't made to hold that weight—
a little sky, but not so much of it.
Not so much that the skin unfolds its silver skeleton
and the joints bend backwards.

And the chemistries that have been devised
to look like water, but to burn like solar heat—
to slip along our fiber canopy and find your flesh—

or the metal canisters whirling through the streets
like old soup cans, spilling smoke
that drifts into your mouth to leave you blind and choking,
a throat burning with manufactured fevers—

Well. Of course an umbrella offers little comfort
where there is drought and darkness.
We really only cover faults in construction
and standard usage as defined.

Therefore, we regret to tell you that there will be no
 refunds or replacements.
In such circumstances, your loss was inevitable.
No warranty could cover it.

Anatomy, Part One

I. (Dentistry)

This is the place where all nourishment
      begins, the love affair
      after the passion, a middle-aged
      marriage where life begins to be broken down
into something we can accommodate.
Ah, now you understand, how the stones
      rise brave as whitewashed houses
      across the pink hills,
a landscape that recedes and swells in the weather,
pressed from behind by a muscle
      that creates a language.
I have once again surrendered the blunt bricks
to white coated strangers,
      to whistling instruments, scaffolding,
a grid of tiled and textured sky
      that goes on and on and on.
It seems like a futile investment, really—
      drilling into the foundations to keep
      walls standing, the life
coming in with its pieces, pointless
when there is no one who is not a number
      in one way or another.
So much maintenance, these old things.
      Still, even with the flaking enamel, these walls
will be the hardest of all of them to destroy.
They are measured, counted out, recorded—
      the only way that others will recognize me
after all of the rest has gone.

II. (Ribs)

We will hold you in, keep you
where you should be,
hang you near your source,
the inverse flow, the ocean that
becomes the tributaries,

then the streams, then the springs
dripping underground. Breathe easy.
See, our fingers have no joints
and cannot bend, won't crush you,
can only curve in a cradle around
the slow-dance that marks
the circle of your swaying.
We only mean to keep our charges
where they are meant to stay.
When Jonah was in the fish he looked up
to see outside the whale's stomach
the sloping white rafters that kept
its flesh from collapsing in.
He was heartened by the way they stretched
toward heaven in the darkness,
felt the wild urge to start a fire
but was stifled by a cough,
carbon expectation trying to twist out.
We have been there too,
halves that rest in black,
one side hearing the comfort of the other,
with your softness struggling warm between us.
We are content without touching,
but fear we will someday lie bare and arched
still staring, reaching but
without you there.
It doesn't matter that we have been divided before,
from other versions of ourselves,
out of some other, longer-lived body,
and know that separation is not always the end.
Once joined, who doesn't worry about the
         unjoining?

III. (Lungs)

         Learn to call to your beloved
the way that others have before you,
sending their sighs into green branches
where they crackled like wrappers.
Drop a song from your mouth unbeautifully

when you're the only one at home.
Whisper someone else's secret
in a crowd of voices.
　　　Sometimes your exhalation is the glow of steam
and its fade, a swipe across the beaded mirror,
but sometimes it snaps, cold like a trap
around the forepaw of a fox.
You have measured so much by it,
betrayed your temperatures.
You've risen up prayers like loaves of bread.
You have let your call ring through the air
like a shot to graze an ear, and then apologized
to any who heard it. Your carbon dioxide has fed the grasses.
If you've called for help as much as from hunger—
both of them start the same way.
A mother's heart was farther from you
　　　　than it had ever been.
Like God's exhalation into Adam
they hit your soles with good intentions
and filled you up enough to cry.

IV. (Grip)

Peel the potatoes with the
peeler, not a knife, she told us.
A knife can take off
too much skin. Peel away
from you, away from others.
Make sure the potatoes are
clean before you put them in
the pot, that the eyes have
been worried out into pits.
Knead the egg and flour into one
idea, away from you, knead
it further, push it out,
pull it back. Roll it with a
pin until it's flat.
Don't touch your face
with flour on your hands.
Wear gloves when you scrub

68

the sink with Comet. Don't slip
holding sharp objects.
People rely on you, she told us.
This is what you were made
to do. If these knuckles dry
out, they will crack into
the pans. If they hit too hard
they could split, show their
ivory-knobbed faces
outside of the caress that
is their home.
If it happens, it will hurt.
It takes a long time
to get those fingers back in.

White Noise

Suddenly there's that opening inside, a cold place.
I don't remember it happening. The images I remember
A dream, not concrete, no horizon line, but gray soft like fur.
How I couldn't believe I would see past morning congealed
Like gelatin, the day was a fog with the outlines of barns, cars
Making noise on a white road. When you had no dark and golden
Flavor left in you, all sunk out. What sun could rise on you lying
In the grass, burning in your shape? The open eyes, flat, bright mud.
Once home. The windows have turned mirrors, thistles and clouds
Sticking to brown Nothing, no one looking out—the agoraphobic
Has made his escape. Welcome, he hears, to the place without prayer,
Where the summer dew seeps past the god-lies in the locked room.
Not a single possession stolen from me in the absence, just the silence
I knew how to spend. Beside that chinchilla-soft shape I stand
Watching the earth fill itself back in, trying to feel the change
In elevation. The one place I wouldn't allow you to get to.

III. Light and Heat

Lesson on a Friesian

We were strangers but agreed on enough.
The trot flung me onto the neck at first,
like being tossed from a shadowed room
into a night sharp with dark intelligence.
So I sat back and settled into it.
The black rushed up to points
through which I saw trees standing
up and down the sky at the arena gates.
The gait traveled us, slow and high;
the spurs on my heels sang like bells at a marriage.
We trotted into dust when we turned,
and the trainer called out to give her more rein.
Afterwards my legs ached for three days
while the mare went on existing in her sunny field,
black hooves lifting her up like stone plates,
onyx eyes buried up to buffalo grass,
and the sun melting into the shining coat
while she forgot all of which we had spoken.

What Followed Me Home

I know how sometimes what you've worn hangs on,
how you can still be too temperatured after
shrugging out, shoulders loose
from losing heaviness and snow.

The drapings of economy and conscience
hang in layers, imperfect credit,
the sins of the fathers, the bad divorce,
evidence of last year's cold

in shreds of Kleenex, and restaurant peppermints
cellophane-sticky in the pocket.
Folds of stale coffee and other old nourishments
spread soft as oil to stain your sleeves.

Most of the year here is sunny enough
to keep me out of my outerwear.
But often even now, I wear something
like a coat.

After the Blood Moon

A thousand years before, I would have feared
to take my eyes from it,

as if my attention were all that stood between
the mountains and destruction.

The red tint would have seemed an omen
of the fall of kings or kingdoms.

I would listen in the darkness
for a messenger of bad news,

think the shadows on the surface
were the places where the blood simmered

in its distress, and were meant for me. For us.
I would keep vigil until the morning hours

for fear of not waking again once asleep.
I would light a fire and feed the fire all it wanted.

When the dogs growled at each other beyond the fire,
I would not think that they were playing

but turning into their wilder selves.
Surely any woman who had a child then

would feel it destined for darkness.
The way the logs crackled and snapped

would seem like the voices of war.
Everything that came before

would seem to have fulfilled a prophecy.
And all the next day, I would see signs

in the restlessness of the horses twitching their skin,
the color of autumn light and paleness of its shadows,

the erratic flight of city birds, and a sound, far away, like a shot.
Even the grass seems different on a day like that,

standing in sharp relief against the sun, every blade up.
The hours would move on restlessly,

and in the weariness of my diligence
I would start to forget to keep watch.

Later, when twilight began to fall again
I would remember the night before,

how, when it seemed the earth trembled as it split into pieces,
my neighbors had howled into the sky,
then laughed,

and how I thought for certain then that God
had finally done with men.

There is a Cry in the Room

There is a cry in the room for which words
have never mattered. I hear their shapes in
deepening corners. There is the suicide of Van
Gogh, the awful being aware of the strength in
a finger, the malicious aloneness of a wheat-field
abruptly heavy with not at rest or moving;
there is the thrust of wings against my palm;

Darkness is a song without trees or unburdened air. I count
the tines of light where nothing was, but the sky could not hold
anything else. Above me I am whistling: someday I will not think
in terms of "remarkably bright" or "solid as"; ankles, birds that are
not still, Parisian women shaking the rain from their overcoats:

There are the faces that I pass, all mine in the
night, and my histories, and everything here looks
dimly familiar, sheathed in that strange silence.

In mirrors, my ear is gone—the sun is gone, slipping
off our skin,
leaving no accusations, only our names.

There is that forgotten in my throat, that feeling that
quiet is the measure of sound.

Always, that the stars have not gone surprises me.
They had pressed against my hands like
something meaning not to stay

Middle Aging

Like a homeland in which I have never seen the attractions,
I am unknown but familiarly named.
It takes ages for the bath to get hot enough to settle into,
comfortable once it reaches the temperature of a fever.
My skin, this age for the first time,

used to be spotless pink in the ceramic kitchen sink
where my mother, thinner, with longer, darker curls,
 poured plastic cup rivulets over no-tears shampoo.
The water was never too cold then, and the suds lifted
in dimensional rainbows that burst against the counter.
With each cupful she told me
to close my eyes, and keep them closed.

I worry now that the old soap around the sides
will betray the form that my hours are becoming.
That there is so much more space to fill.
I don't recognize the lines on hands I should know,
start to feel strange aches, have cancer scares.
I long to stay anywhere long enough to sink in and soak,
call in sick to work without being sick,
but there is too much to do, and a price for survival.
The water drops by half when I step out to dress,
dripping mummy in a frayed gray towel.

Strange to remember when I wasn't allowed to be naked alone for long,
waiting for her warnings not to splash too hard or slip.
Too much time in the water is dangerous, she would say,
will wrinkle your knuckles into old plums. You could fall asleep.
Belly down, you could drown. Even two inches is deep enough to do it.

Flats

From the first night, that apartment
nearly finished us: the avocado stains in
damp corners, unforgiving odor of stale yeast,
the leaking gas that the landlord bribed us to conceal,
a death-trap. But it was cheap and all we had,
and we lived there making our rent.

Because he made the money then,
he could say, *A woman wears three inches.*
I left my old flats one at a time
so none of them could get lost together,
and no one else could put them on.
The scent of the whiskey that made him unreason
drifted out and in with his sleep.

Those shoes were gone and there was nothing left
to buy new ones, ones to go out in,
so I walked on the heels of bread
baked fresh before he got home,
expecting to capsize on the fingers
of loose orange frieze, or
trip on the carpet tacks where the pad was thin.
While I checked the hot oven my hair swung
for the cat to bat at with a paw.

That was home then.

Buttermilk

I found myself on hands and knees
in the kitchen, cleaning as if it were all I knew,
an unbothered Bessie in a field of fences
unaware of my own stomachs.
The tags in my ears drooped
like wet sheets, and milk skinned
until it was skimmed.
I lived on grass and water
and thought all were of my kind.

I did not think about it until there was a dry year,
the year the fires tried to burn us all on our feet.
Guided by the charred posts
we walked miles with covered faces,
before men on horses who allowed us to hold
onto our lowing calves
while we were driven at the edges
and the copper pots clanged.

How could we tell who sought to save us,
or who wanted to drive us to our deaths?
Let me tell you, once I was wise
I bellowed through those
gray alloys of catastrophe as fast as I could,
though I was breathing ash.
I took the first gate that called when the lips opened
from the road to a bare patch of ground.

After the tragedy
the days were the same.
I was nowhere unusual
and I was nosing aching plants.
I didn't pay much attention
to what I was chewing in my cud.

Before I realized it I was making butter again,
and sweeping, and all the old habits,
never a hair's breadth late to table,

80

placid in my expectations and
waiting for boots to sound the hand-scraped pine.

Which of us was born not wanting to please?
It takes more than past disasters
to change the way a woman fears.

Grand Canyon

I.

The day you left the light was blood-sticky.
Leaves hanging lazily in the heat, the sweat seeping through my shirt,
the smell of grease on concrete, thick brown with sand caught in it,
radiating waves of heat.

The hot congealed sand. You pulled the cries from me.

Did you know it when we met? Did you?
Every year I got sicker.

My knees unstuck and the ground unstuck into my hair.
You pulled me along the yard while the neighbors stared.
My elbows came all undone.

II.

Noise of cars turning corners, the light mild like a rosary,
dogs padding, the gravel feathery earthiness, cigarette butts.
Sometimes children.

Who can guess how many of them there were going to be.
We had the same fat knees, the same wheat hair.
The questions now are the color of their eyes,
the shapes of their noses, how tall they would be.
The little clouds of their words that would hang
in the air when they played in the cold,
their fingers making pictures on windows as the houses went by.

They do not now have the right to breathe.
Their mother sits on benches smiling absentmindedly,
watching buses and seasons,

Fingering red apples dusty with their coating of wax.
We learned what only you could teach us:

ghosts make better company.

III.

Green and chalk that summer, the kind of green that
means more rain fell than usual, more gnats in the air.
A yellow autumn, because we had no trees, only grass
shrinking into its roots, and ants engineering tunnels. A lot of living
undone.
Terracotta summer, without any mud.
Grey again that spring and a lot of living undone.

There was a canary that year, and his unconquerable
belief kept the house bright with song.
(We were always finding keys that didn't belong to any locks,
and wasps somehow kept getting into the rooms).

The canary sang as if he were home, his sound like wind
blowing snow from wild places in the heights—we were always
smelling pine trees in our yard of desert.

I learned lessons that only you could teach me:
the freedom in mistakes. An ache as natural as hunger.
The way words could wrap us in silence.

Did you know? Religion gives up on you. It radiates limits.
His song circled like light,
round enough to put shadows in the corners.
The way the streetlight throws circles on the ground,
points of campfires through the wilderness,
the reaching orbits of stars.

That spherical glow.

Every Judas from the time the first pagan sang up the sun
Has become you.
The horizon is the same in every direction,
all of them round from far enough out.

You could never reach the end.

But the canary doesn't know.
He still wants to find her.
He will radiate what he can.
Sing, sing, sing.
Make a place for the seeing to stop.

IV.

There is a pin in
(Anguish for himself)

To categorize what fluttered.
(No pity for that which he killed)

Their wings spread flat in
(Your body blocks the light)

A catalogue of flight.
(I didn't plan on swimming back)

We label what is displayed.
(It could be sleeping)

To think of the things that used to scare me
(The things that scare me now).

V.

Did you know did you know did you know did you?
In my mind they have become one woman,
A white hand with chewed fingernails, an arm that is brown,
An olive ankle that a buckle has bitten into, dark breasts,
Mismatched hips, a dark and a hazel eye,
Hair twisting nervous like her fingers.

My landscape is scarred with years of you.
You thought you had looked everywhere, but
There are still secrets. You were your own guide.

You didn't find all the shimmering valleys
You didn't find the forests that whispered stories
You didn't find the mighty river that drew roots to it
You found some but you didn't find them all.

Snow fell in the canyon and had fallen for a while
by the time I arrived to look over the edge.
The fog thickened and stuck but I couldn't rub it off.
I thought about how I came so far to see white. To see
The old yearning and know I had no place to keep it.

At the overlook rain fell. The figures huddled with no expression
Under dark coats. I looked out because they did.
It was the vastness breathing out of something we couldn't see,
The muffled flat of our voices.
The nothing was bigger than anything we had known before.

She was less beautiful than I am, but you didn't think so.
She was less loved than I am, but you loved her more.
If that is not the death of us, it is this:

You gave your silver to that calico woman, for her to hide
in the faded folds of mismatched clothes.

And did you know.

Did you know what I thought
the first time I saw this place?

I thought that they must have buried God here.

Why I Stopped Keeping a Journal

Words were the last possession he took from me when he left,
as if giving me his name had given him the right to what was mine.
They were one more item to add to the list of what I lost:
fifteen pounds, my favorite sweater, photographs, a baby,
finally my words in blue ink, that nightly ritual of hand-writing,
proof of what mistakes we had made and what I was afraid of (him).
He showed them to his mother, his sisters, his friends, his therapist.
The other women wondered why he carried his wife with him that way.
I know why he took my journal, book of six years of bruises and
          brandy-breath:
it is the only place we still live in the home he threw away.

He won't turn past the last filled page to the clean emptiness of afterlife.
He keeps my journal, document of six years of bruises.
The other women wonder why he carries his former wife with him that
way.
He shows my words to his mother, his sisters, his friends, his therapist—
proof of the mistakes we made and what I was afraid of (him).
My own words in blue ink, that nightly ritual of hand-writing:
fifteen pounds, my favorite sweater, photographs, a baby,
one more item to add to the list of what was lost.
I threw away his name, the one possession he left me with.
That word, which was his own, was what I gave him when I left.

Miscarriage

Some suffering changes the shape of things,
cuts a chasm between now and what came before.
You arrive in the strange country that loss brings.

The sparrow's broken body, its backward-bent wing,
will still try the flight that lives at its core:
it doesn't know its pain changes the shape of things.

The abandoned wife knows, twists off her ring,
and teaches it to live in her bedside drawer.
She arrives in the strange place that loss brings.

Even outside the hospital, the chemo clings
in hair on a shirt, and the blood count keeps score.
Some suffering changes the shape of things.

Take just one second back. The pendulum swings
back and hangs. A molester unopens the door.
No one wakes in the strange room that loss brings.

You can't fix it with tape or tie it back on with string.
You remember a place you can't get to anymore.
Some suffering changes the landscape of things:
she almost lived. Still lives in the space that loss brings.

Dark Canyon

Gnats hummed in the reeds, and flies that looked like bees
colored the mud of the soft bank. We were watched
by what we saw, brown shadows in the water
throwing dull highlights filtered through needle and stream and smell
to long cool muscles sliding
        off the current.

Between fallen wire and undergrowth we came to a place no one had
stood. From there I made my cast, drifted,
        and from that dark and cold
we tricked them into biting,
that those naked grubs and salmon eggs
were the stream's. Not outsiders, but their own,
fallen from their trees, born by their kind.

I didn't feel the change.
The line caught, that was all, a moss-covered branch or old lure.
But what came in glinted iridescent rainbow and had mute eyes
banded with gold.
        A hook wrenched its gut; it had swallowed the lie.

In the roaring of the boulders we could not discuss
how to treat the problem of the fish.
You pulled with its mouth gaping but pain held. The staring eyes could
not lose much of their expression in death.
Finally its suffering grew too much for us so you scraped the soul
out with your knife.

There was a climb back to the road in which my feet seemed far from
        me.
Suddenly it was not a fish. There was no majestic and cold world
filled with tides, or the taste of snow in the water.
        Not even a memory of the sky
flickering, the sun in passing trees and lazy dragonflies,

sleep caught in eddies by the rocks, waiting to see morning,
the vitality of keeping the air and earth
                holding us between them.

In that dark heat of ownership, I knew.

They Gather Their Belongings

(in response to the photograph of the Syrian refugee child found
dead on the beach)

They know what many will never study,

like how to press olives into soft thinness
that melts over the tongue,

and how to make goat's milk into cheese.

How to make something into bread.

How to eat when they have to pretend
that something is enough.

How to let the walls shake, if they must.

How to quiet children between the blasts
and comfort the baby when it wakes to rubble.

How to tell the difference between
a home that will kill them
and a house that might let them live.

How to gather their belongings.

How to make something— anything— into a boat.

How to bring their children with them to the sea.

How to go into the sea with them bundled.

How to tell them stories of the sea.

How bright are the bundles,
and the sea is unfathomable and cold.

How it tosses the craft that they have fashioned.

89

How to lose their children to the sea.

Though I lost a child once, it was not the same as that.
It was too early for anyone to know it was a child.
It was cells with barely any form.

It was not like the one that they knew.

This one has a red shirt, black hair,
shoes still fastened. This one was perfect.

We know it, when we look at him
pale and perfect, facing away from us
toward the sea that he left.

The way we find him: not facing us.

How we learn to carry him out of the water,
but he does not belong to us.

There are pictures of us carrying him out,
but he still does not belong to us.

Everyone knows it. How bright are the bundles.

We are gathering their belongings.

The sea is unfathomable and cold.

Though I lost a child once, it was not the same as that.

Papa's Armistice

The red and white silk square
with its flags of the Allies and
its faded outline of the Peninsula,
creased with the old wallet's folds
and yellowed with sun,
is the one souvenir
he brought back from Korea.

Shells and carvings, pictures,
war trophies and weapons,
the soldiers bought some of everything
for the people back home.

As the woman took his damp coins
she must have thought of a young wife
waiting to bud on a faraway tree
as she herself was soft hips
under the thin dress starting
to bloom.

How strange to them both that somewhere there
wasn't jungle and water. Even the leaves
either sweated or rained.

The rice paddies too
never rested,
frogs and snakes slipping into canals,
and insects singing
under the fat faces of the prophet.

Maybe she became an old woman,
 who knows? He would not tell us
anything about the war. There was a hole
between the gods and a confusion of
missing brothers there.

 I always wanted to ask him why,
of all that he left there

and all that he walked away from, buried,
he saved the cheap silk picture
of a dripping country's outline,
but I suspect that woman
who didn't hate him, who touched
his hand when he counted out his money,

who stood like a watercolor tiger
in the purple dusk,
was the only way he could come home.

That gaudy scarf was folded so small,
so many times,
to fit into his pocket.

Catch and Release

For once we didn't discover something by what it had left,
though we found evidence of it later
in places that surprised us.

We found half-eaten food in the back of the pantry,
with the packages tattered, plastic wrappers powdered
into the cereal crumbs. There was beat-up drywall
in out-of-the-way places along the baseboards.

What gave it away was a relentless gnawing in the walls,
when we'd wait in bed to fall asleep,
not as if something scratched at the outside to come in,
or tried to burrow outside from where we were,
but as if it were digesting the house from the roof down,
untidily, for no good reason. It was hard to live

there knowing the house was coming down around us.
So we set our traps along the wall and waited.
When we caught it we were sorry about its trembling,
the fur that lay finely along its spine,
its eyes bright and aware of what we stood for.
But it couldn't stay with us. Who knows
if it survived long where we released it,

the first field we came to that wouldn't impose on any neighbors,
where we last saw it scrambling over chunks of hard earth
that had been freshly plowed,
and the sky seemed so open to danger?

The rough arches of its entry have been patched,
and steel wool plugs places around the pipes.

There is no more gray dash in our rooms
when we turn on the lights early
and step into a space we weren't expected.

The walls are as quiet as we are.

You always hear that where one is,
there will be more, but we have noticed none,
although each of us has been looking ever since.

Holiness

Teeth can close on an arm
or around a warm throat.
There's the serrated edge of the bear-trap,
the sing of the snap as it closes on paws.

I always thought I would trade my own hand
to sing well, but now I wonder
what I would do with it—
just stand in the choir with everyone else
who can sing?

Our voices are like mermaids, coming
from below a green pool, from someplace clear
into someplace hot, blameless fish breaching into woman,
everything always in that spot
between water and sky.

We shall cry sanctuary and
learn how to hide.

Did you hear it?—believe
in the steadfastness of stone,
that appetites can gnaw the
shell without breaking through.

Thousands of people greater and more afraid
than I am have watched the fight through these windows.

A church is echoes and answers of whispers. Pews
stretch unassuming on a stone floor,
reaching out to one another,
an orchard of trees that touch fingers just long enough
to make shade and seeds

Three Flights

I.

You pretend the walls are boundaries,
but there's the noise of another shower running.
The smell of what someone else eats.
The sound of the family next door praying
near the open window
while you wait on your balcony.

II.

You know someone has left for good
if you happen to see, when you come up the stairs,
a door left open to the shampooed carpet
of an empty dining room.
Or, if your car is blocked in one morning by a moving van.
Or if you stop hearing the couple downstairs
cursing at each other in the parking lot.

It doesn't mean anything
if the pink bicycle always chained to the stairwell disappears—
it could have just been stolen.

III.

Birds sometimes come in through the vents in the building.
Last year, I found a sparrow in the middle of my living room.
I picked it up in a grocery bag turned inside-out.
It was warm and limp, and must have just stopped breathing.

That doesn't happen only to me.
        I once walked by a vacant apartment
where the painters had left the blinds up.
A grackle beat itself against the window
and watched the strangers passing through
a pale reflection of its crashing heart.

Five Years After It Ended

The truth is that I never think of you.
I don't recall your lies or their octaves.
It would be nice if you forgot me too,

duct-taped and discarded like the work boots
you wore the heels out of. It's so hard to forgive,
the truth is I just stopped thinking of you.

It took a long time, like when rusted screws
strip loose from the splintered post where they were captive.
It would be nice if you forgot me too.

People trusted your rough hands. No one knew
how the temper smoldered under that sunbeat skin, furtive.
The truth is that I rarely think of you.

Under ice, the trees shook. Spring, and they grew.
I stopped worrying you'd find where I live.
It would be best if you forgot me too.

By the way, the letters you sent never got through.
When all has been said, there's no more motive:
so send no more. I barely think about you.
Stay out of my houses, and forget me too.

IV. The Way It Radiates

The Funeral's Last Guest

I have been both the burier and the one being buried—
the one left for dead on roadsides and in ditches
when the cold should turn breath white enough to see,
and the one throwing dirt over what I have cared for
once it has stilled.

The last time I died, I lay there and listened.
The dirt hit the lid like the slap of a sprinkler's spray
on a house as the head oscillates by.
If there had been a bell, I would have sounded it.
It was like waiting in the darkness of a marriage,
a barely-big-enough box I was given
because I was loved enough.
When I started to claw out,
I knew it would hurt.

When I do the burying,
I use old shoeboxes, ones I keep under the bed just in case.
They smell like silica gel.
I dig holes under trees
so that their roots will comfort what has been killed
and support some of my burden.

When I leave, I look back, shovel in hand.
I wonder if anyone else will find the graves.

No matter what I bury, how it differs every time,
something about it is always the same.

What Bees Know

In the beginning, you uncurl
yawning out of the darkness soft like an infant
          from your warm cocoon.

Even newly unshielded,
you are wise enough to see
          that nothing is yours,

not even your nursery or nest.
You will unfold your beating wings soon,
slow dance through the crowd in the basement

and say where the flowers are—
          you'll lead them weaving
through fields shaggy with horses

and take sweetness where you can get it
          (it is not stealing if you know
that something could never really be yours).

All day you will dedicate yourself
to the comfort of your craft,
then rest quietly humming,

          breathing out the honeyed dark
with your sisters.
You will know that you have

made something good, drawn out and holy
          like praise from the mouth
of a monarch.

You know well enough to be efficient
at what you do.
          Do it while you can.

Someday your family will call you out;
there will be some great need for your defenses.
You will unsheathe your weapon

and forget it in the beekeeper's hand.
      You'll find that night is the nectar
      and dark is a bloom

that guides you back in.

Solstice

When the winter voices begin to drop
from branches, we make
scarecrows to keep them from alighting
near us.

Words went out but never back in.
We breathed each other's prayers
as they spread like sails on the coarse paper air.

Our hands were in our pockets and our numb
fingers could not warm each other.

The cold has bled also into more solid borders,
frosting the edges in patterns of impact;

seeping past the ribs which suspend
the ground, solid beneath us though the ship heaves.

It gave our walk its shape, those ghosts beneath waiting.
This sleep from which we were made, vaguely remembered.

The sea presses the rooms where those staring bones are kept,
sailors who have grown too honest.

The chains of their last bondage push up the earth
and our vessel creaks.

There are memories here that haunt. Reminders of the laughter
when home was entire, and the ribs did not cause concern.

The kitchen table, the way the windy wheat looked
from the dusty window as curtains breathed though the panes
were closed. The house we imagined, as real as blood.

We are unchangeable in our places,
though the stone aches. I have heard you sigh,

arms outstretched to the changing moons, bearing no expression,
only weather.

Wild geese cried as they took to wing, as they do now,
their wake leaving ice that melts from old trees
whose roots go deep enough to hear myths of spring.

The ground claims what has fallen, its tribute
for keeping us aloft.

Beside us, our shadows are flung on the white.

Streetlights at dusk wake on a road where no one walks,
throwing light in case someone comes.

For Days Now

For days now, I have sought news of her,
have become the eavesdropper of peripheral voices
and the absent keeper of white
waiting-room hours, have been an inquisitor
of mutual friends, but only a few,
have searched my imaginings through views that opened
onto tree-muted windows and
the smudged brass edges of knobs
that reveal beds of *prognoses* and *malignance*,
words that spread out, leaves alighting on water
to ripple smaller and open through the rocks
of impolite questions. I have thought
many times of the feeling of
the overlapping ghosts of dried
mornings that progressed in rings of coffee,
a reverberation of candor, where she often
laughed at how silly we were,
but that has been years now.

Though they told me of the cancer
I tried to forget, an easier way to undo the loss,
to pretend that I've never seen such sickness play out.
If I have not heard otherwise I can think
I have not waited too long to find her,
that someday we are not all pulled past the muddy bank
into an atmosphere that suffocates with some glory
for which our breath is unprepared.

Days now. I have thought about how,
for a while, we are netted in the wake of memory,
a lesson my grandmother teaches,
calling me her absent daughter, or her sister's name,
for a moment thinking the face she knew in youth
was mine.

There are still no new emails today.
As the air rings with the charged
white static of this silence,
I wonder the best time to call.

How to Paint a Pièce de Résistance

You must travel among uncased violins
as the city passes in a blur
of childlike impressions.
Chagall should sit a few seats in front,
his loneliness
a flea market of color.
The seats should wear their old passengers
bared with yellow styrofoam.

The carnival music must waft in. Not yet,
but before too long. The air will
turn thick to hold the trapeze.
You should try to hide your knowledge
of the exile toward which you run.
The artist, frantic before his deconstruction,
should absorb the pastel voices like hot afternoon
letting sound fall in on itself,
before he sneaks
trailing oils off the train.

He might try to tell us, I can't stop waking as myself,
that sort of wide and lonely walk
littered with pigeon feathers and graffiti.
Try to get out of this one, the Tents fluttering
as they pyramid the sea breeze.
Our meeting is only a chance one.

If you didn't expect to recognize anyone
it would be different.
If you avoid questions you can finish a masterpiece,
riding off into your work mouthing the violin
while the paint streams
down some horse's round haunches.

Wind-tossed against the carousel, the torn posters
always promote past acts.
The salt in this air corrodes and caresses.
He never does say goodbye.

    : Become famous and keep on painting.

Horsehead Nebula

I found a horse before he was only bones,
before his warmth dissolved
in empty sockets.

Laid out empty, it was like
he was a vessel from which to drink.
It was a grasp to see it wasn't mine.
I kicked his forehead to wake him,
a sound of watermelon-hollow.
Bright chestnut and flax stilled,
the vacant eyes like an old woman's.

Solar flare: the phone rings once.
What was magnificent waits to be disposed.
I'm still counting your theories of age.

In this sea of stars, there is a clot:
Cosmic eccentricity.

The Waffle House Near Midnight

Fact: 95 cent coffee. The menu proclaims it
and plates of eggs and grits. No hungry travelers.
I thought about trying the raisin toast,
a quiet meal late in the evening, full of cinnamon.
Drink refills are free, tables sticky,
our heads a mass of truth and
Fact: our menus are also our placemats.
The absurdity of the clock behind your head
sweeping time up with its hands and dropping it,
feigning dignity (what dignity is there in
time? which always runs away or hides)
makes me think,
I could own a diner like this, always open.
The girl in the red sweater
pushed the door when it said "pull,"
shook herself out of the shame,
and stepped through. She is behind us;
there's a survey of the ketchup marks on the china,
potatoes that slid onto the table.
The window reflects blue eyes, the red vinyl, the linoleum floor,
Cassiopeia knocking to be let in, the old ATM machine;
pushes us up into the dark glare of glassy shine outside,
makes of us colored constellations.
Fact: we are the number one server of hash browns
and
the night falls into the windows. Coffee
can be the best distraction.
Fact: our pancakes dwarf Mount Everest
Fact: three kinds of pie

When the ISS Exits the Shadow

At 6:18, a light appears over the landfill to the west
just as NASA said it would,
one of the brightest points in the sky,
not blinking like a plane or cell tower,
or falling the way a meteorite falls,
but smooth and strong, a star that moves faster than the other stars
in an irrevocable arc,
immaculate spider swinging once across the roof of the night:
the International Space Station.
I have no coat on, though it is Christmas and cold,
and a line from Wilbur rings in my head
though it isn't a different month yet, but soon, something like
the new year, whose bells will wrangle with the snow
a song that circles around your hopes once you hear it—

The star that isn't a star has been visible for two minutes now.
Watching it feels almost secret, like driving by a neighbor's house
when they have forgotten to close their blinds before dark,
and for a second they are visible as they eat in their living room,
hunched over their plates and waiting to be filled

And attached to the light, its few lonely people
are living healthily within it, far removed from us,
either awake or asleep, but if awake, seeing the darkened half
of our brilliance of blues and greens below them.

They can't stop us. They could watch us set fire to ourselves and do
         nothing,
immune from our bad decisions, live on until starvation takes them
months after our existence on earth has ended

Something like this, flashing through its orbit indomitable
as the memory of a first love, says someone is safe from us,
even if our deaths would someday mean theirs too,
and the same light will someday spark with no one to see it,
the souls of our only survivors clanging against its hatches
and bouncing back—

At 6:23, the light dims and disappears
in its arc, fades like an ember that leaves a ghost when your eyes close.
It took just five minutes to travel across my line of sight,
exactly the way I had been told that it would.

The Desert Forgets

The desert forgets, though we leave our mark
In the struggle against ending alone.
Even daylight's fierce heat fades to the dark.

Who cultivates sand may call it a park
Pure as Eden, and feel that he is home.
The desert forgets, though we leave a mark.

A brief glint in the night, the sacred spark,
The nomad's fire that burns back the unknown:
A soft stain of heat that fades in the dark.

Fear crouches without. Walls keep us apart
And give us a place. Outside the wolves moan.
The desert forgot, though we left our mark.

The crow's wings, from below, gleam green as a lark's.
He sees the bending of what we have grown,
Those dull stones of progress that fade in the dark.

Watch them come blinking as they disembark,
And hide what the wind finds (white point of bone).
The desert forgets, though we leave our mark—
Children of the heat that fades in the dark.

Dystopia

In movies, the future always seems bleaker
the longer it will take to arrive.
Dark -sunned, overgrown with ivy,
it is a wilderness of trees thrusting through the buildings
of large and well-known stone metropolises,
while the highways splinter and fall to pieces
under the skeletons of minivans. In the poisoned air,
the cracked landscape is as full of shadows
as a room without windows.

There, people don't seem like themselves.
The rules have changed. Or there are no rules.
Martial law. Sometimes there has been a plague,
and people lie under white sheets in echoing hallways.
There are conscious machines all over the city,
indifferent as sickness themselves,
made of invincible alloys, ruthless
because they don't love.

We are shown again and again
that we will cause our own destruction,
like Romans, unconquered but falling
in on ourselves.

Maybe it's true that we'll end up
that way, or worse. You hear everyone saying
that the world is going downhill fast.
It's one disaster after another: wars, hunger.
Foundations are still looking for cures.
The same stories are on the evening news.

Recycled explosions. Each beginning,
like the day you met your first heartbreak,
when you were a blank screen that could have been filled
with anything. When you learned to pretend
that something could look new

over and over again.

Physics of the Curve

If we are moving, we must be falling.
But not so fast we notice yet. It's a slow sink,
like drink, then drunk; the curves that draw us in. The bead of

condensation sweating
down a bottle—you can't

help but watch it slip to a wet ring
on the hardwood stain. Dimmer switch
of sun-slide. The sighing down

to supernova while we kick the round waves
of salt-licked vistas and enjoy the weather. This orbit
should blow us right off our feet, I've heard,
straight to the crater moon, lunar
halo whitening its blind side,

but gravity is greedy,
tries to pull us under, is not without a fight.
It seems we are always in-between.
Our cold and billowing atmosphere
sits anchored on its tether until it
gets too full and has to dive, so

it clears out, driving without
any sort of question rain
to mud, and not surface-stopping,

unwinding underground caverns, Ogallala
pools under houses,
but skyward it doesn't make a sound,
just a rush or roar or drumming when
it has come into contact with the ground,
and the thrill of a burst, a bubble under,
some other place it can make it through.

Our kind of falling is in love, hard, out
of grace, free, to the floor, back

at least once a year, we name a season for it,

get shorter every summer
as our mass drags us toward the middle,
sparking children closer
to the center than ourselves. But
it's never fast enough.
The slant goes back as far as we can see,
ringing the years like a redwood.
At this rate we will go on falling bit-by-bit forever,
though our end has always seemed so soon.

The tide goes back. A space is made for water
somewhere. I still don't feel my age,
could wait as long as it takes to find out

if down is the only direction.
The gathering weather grows
heavy, cracks its lid, sloshes out the cold drops.
It has always been this way.
Heaven shivers into a sea solid enough to slip

below its astral arch.
It falls, it hits. It slips out
like the curve from someone's motherhood.
It tells a thirsting ground
about its sciences.

Adam

It is the rib, not what lies under it, that
aches. The wound is strange, the strange blood is hot
as it rises against the walls, rushing to itself.

Summer heat moves houseplants and air
rubs quietly with the hum of the fan, bright blades
rolling like hawks over a still landscape,

the desert in their skylit eyes and the cry
that drops to columns (*Can this be
mine? Can this...*), a blur the colorless desert that
engraves the palms of callused hands,
presses sand into stone with its weight.

It is the asymmetry: ivies move—the tedious fan—
people talk in other houses; the heat lifts hair with
sticky wind, tangles with the smell of oranges.

The mountain sleeps above the family, capless. Martinique
sleeps, its terrier sleeps trotting the grey street
past the texture of frozen faces in an old morning (*leaves
in sunlight leaves in sunlight sky-branches sunlight sunlight*).

Dusk and blackbirds spread, to a sleeping
town the paper sound of wings, throb of lullabies
caught in the air above the cradle, from somewhere the
roomless noise of running water down old chimneys.

Below the in-between trees and the red mud of the river,
the bones are unlistened-for, unsung together.
Ancient hands disunite rock; fingers slide into the white burden.

Silently, the fan moves air around its place. There are apple peels
        and the
empty skins of lemons, curls of zest, and dreaming finches.

Narcissan suns hang to the Mediterranean, touch the hollow
under-skin (*do you know that you are missing? do you recognize*)

116

The waves reach into each other and swell.

His is the unquiet name, the name that is not his own.
(People talk in houses: *can this be mine?* And touch their faces)

He names them and wakes to see the heart uncovered everywhere,
with no bone over it, sandal-less barefoot vacant toes,
unlooked-for as knowledge to him.

Spring Plowing

We remember our rites in time to break ground. Between
teases of rain, the field acknowledges us into its confidence;
the wind slips by us a sliding snake-belly, and we turn to
vibration in the dawn unshattered quiet.

The blue tractor is land-locked, dragging its fingers through rich
earth. The smell dark, fresh, secret. Our hands are soft with the dust
sighing back on our clothes and in our mouths,
leaving meditations where we held the wheel.

In sudden upset the Johnson and ryegrass bury ignoble heads. Indian
paintbrushes cry their yellow and red surrender to the silver grill and
grinning headlights that spoke of peace to them.

From this seat over the tires I can watch the treads back to where
we entered, the barn where the horses lulled their
hay and shook flies from their ears. Before that, the engines slept,

mechanical skeletons empty-headed through white dream winter.
And earlier, there was the bright-spotted Beginning, where Adam
showed his sons how to try to bring back Paradise.

Dogs bark at it and its civilized disquiet, the friendly yellow dog
frightened, the grey indifferent dog a tame wolf with gold eyes.
The orange flowers simply bow to the blue tractor. Fire ants scramble
in their soft ravished tunnels, warm and homeless.

The engine's tongue leaves no room for
noise. Sunlight warms shoulders where the shield of straw hats
breaks. Beside the warm droning and the pollen-dusted faces,
lazy dragonflies turn azure in a fancy of afternoon storms.

This reign is our kingdom. Rows settle and the field closes under the
blue tractor. This spring, a harvest—not a fallow year. With each

pass, we set down lines for the seeds to lie in.

Mahogany

Warm wood reflects the edge of fire, shows
Me bending in my chair to read, then looking up
To see the slightness of the glow hiding in the curve.

Oak, cherry, pine. Trees, the stuff of heirlooms,
Kept forever, with no specific assurance, something to be
Cherished, indifferent to value. To me, a worn archive;

To me, waking on a winter morning,
Running down a spiral staircase,
The Beatles, "Let it Be."
Coffee growing cold in the pot,
Watermelons freezing before they are ripe;
The eyes that stare back at me from the TV screen,
My eyes, watching me looking in, watching people behind me
Eating popcorn.
Something suggests to me,
What does it matter if we waste our time,
If we are anything to no one.
The slow blush of the surface by which I base myself.
Lullabies to babies lying still in their cradles.

I can see my face in the wood, my eyes, my skin,
Nothing that I own. I think if I could reach through
I could come up with a splinter, perhaps, of
Something never-changing: the time I ran into it with the
Vacuum cleaner. A bit of the finish that rubbed off
When I kept setting hot cups on it. The piece under the shelf
Where I wrote my name when I was four.

White Noise

Schizophrenic Jeanne D'Arc's eyes were once chips of horizon.
We get wound tight waiting for rain, though we know eventually it
       must come.
Nevertheless she dried out, preserved now under waxy pieces of glass
       and wood.
Le Coeur de la Guerre. Some talismans are harder to find prayers for.

That Departure—Going Through

They will always say it wasn't suicide,
how they found those white lilies at this
time of year, with all of those
unbuttoned white collars and the green throats
pressed open, wanting to be touched;

and there was nothing wrong with cutting
something that seemed to offer itself in that candid way
that the early lilies have.

I like to imagine them forgiving me for not looking
at their faces when they smiled with nectar,

forgiving me for letting their mouths close
without brushing the pollen off of the lips.

I tell myself that maybe the music has come to that spot in
the *Moldau* where the river no longer tumbles, but begins to dance,
or lets another dance for the chance to hear the echoes
of waltzes grow loud in the heart of the water—

a wooden voice half averted, pushing into the current,
demi-death of the river, almost
a kind of redemption: an event without blame.

The flowers give up their tongues as they speak,
bees dying for every affirmation of themselves.

The sky asks if it pressed too heavily on a leaf
that it knew could bruise—
just a finger and thumb rubbing it, getting the dark
green under the nail.

It seems like everything asks,
even the trees that already stretch with answers,
that took those still limbs into their blood
as soon as they felt them decay.

The too-cold weight of the silence at night
suddenly seems the most alive,
and then the light from under doors pushing into
darkness like antennae, solid warmth of someone
behind the unlit glass, and more—temperature
especially real, the thickest, the most opaque,
the brightest, the feeling most next to skin.

The lilies almost remember budding.
They lower their yellow eyes,
wondering if this quiet lapse will always feel like
something that couldn't possibly have walked out,

something that was barely even apart
from laughing during the prayer and leaving the good book open
after the outburst that revealed another door, an exit

Anatomy, Part Two

V. (Murmur)

The antique watch
is wound by hand.
With its tension
it counts down to
its next winding.
And the time will
start to get slow
on the wrist your father
could wrap his hands
around. The sound
throbs in the room
like a question
with no answer
that waits for one.
Some pulse is all
that keeps you tied
to your hunger,
delivers the
air, impulsive
clock-in-clock-out.
When it stops it will
still seem on schedule,
a shivering of palms
and latent workings that
echo, dumb as any other shrouded
ghost in the machine.

VI. (Ankles)

She is always trying to get
the bicycle chain
back onto the teeth of the gears.

VII. (Posturing)

These old walls don't hold up a roof

anymore, though they once must have been
load-bearing. They lean roughened
by the weather, arms out to welcome sparrows.
As generations rose around them
the stones slipped from their crumbling pockets
and the vines grew
from the feet of the doorways, twisting
doggedly, as if they believed
the world could end next week.
The green vines
dragged themselves to the sun.
If only light could make it
to the bottom of the walls,
the place might see that it has grown spotted,
 like an elderly woman's hands, though
we all were pretty enough
at some age.
The ruin slouches beneath the rain,
fattening slowly into sand,
grown used to becoming a landscape.

VIII. (Memory)

I came here so you would remember
me   not as I was, but
          unblemished, and cool as a sidewalk,
new-china smooth.   So that you'd feel
        your home, a place where light   bursts from places
    that no one has been close to, to warm   the grass
where you sit, to   sink out of proximity
        and chill the curling feet of the trees
as they seek me.   As you lay me out
        with my relatives,
        I have finally stopped being a
wallflower.   I have learned to become a guest instead.
        Be careful not to let them
make you into me   too soon.
        The last train
        leaving on the last day is still too soon.
Your prayer sticks to you,   to all the

124

places that you make a home. Wait.
Wait.
When you get here,   we'll make room.

09112001

Unsuspecting tomatoes (half green, almost too green)
ripen on a windowsill. Gentle cows with sleepy eyes watch
the grass sway, and horses flick late summer flies off their
haunches.

The anchormen won't sleep or haven't for eighteen or twenty hours.
Americans everywhere huddle with noses inside the blue light
of Journalism, look at one another trying to understand, taking
anything
(we are in shock, in shock, in terrible shock)

Rome falls, as it has fallen, becoming a ruthless cliché
(Rome always falls, always falls, heavy like
the sky tumbling down, killing firemen, their grey faces)
tourists in the streets with cameras, airplanes, King Kong
swatting at well-meaning helpless pilots.
Questions from the Statue of Liberty, her torch out, smoking,
eyes smooth, unblinking, far-reaching, blank.

What, one man? peering at the news crew, standing alone in the
aftermath of soot, a weed growing in-between slabs of concrete.
"I'm 69, but I can still run," he says, and, eyeing first the sky
then the camera (perhaps he has said too much), he edges away
(people now are so unsure).

"God bless America," they sing. "God bless America."
(And they mean it).

The noble anchormen shift in their seats, wondering about their wives;
they look at their watches, they hackney the facts, they dream
about eating dinner in a recliner, watching *Seinfeld* like nothing
had happened or does or could again.

Torches, burnt torches. New York far enough away,
people on TV walking, not looking at each other, thinking
to themselves, yesterday seems like last year. We never had to
worry then (there were no holes). Store windows open for people
to watch screens playing the events of the morning. ("...the apocalypse,"

the anchors shout. "A horrible tragedy, another Pearl Harbor.")

It is Pompeii, caught breathing, shocked beyond life, forever
frozen, time a casualty. Pompeii, bedded in ash.
And everywhere, plants growing, unbothered Buttercups giving milk,
feeling that as long as she has legs she is alive, dandelions in the
sidewalk, the fresh fall scent of leaves

www.ingramcontent.com/pod-product-compliance
Lightning Source LLC
Chambersburg PA
CBHW022009100426
42736CB00041B/1224